No Excuses!

50+ healthy ways to ROCK lunch and dinner!

stuffed peppers pg. 25

"People make time for what they care about"
- anonymous

By Erin Macdonald, RDN and Tiffani Baccus, RDN

table of contents

Welcome to the No Excuse Zone

Day in and day out, we hear many excuses from our clients about WHY they don't make a homemade lunch or dinner. Do any of these sound familiar?

"I don't have the time!"

"I don't know what to do with the ingredients I have!"

"I have no protein in the fridge so I can't make a meal!"

"I don't want a heavy meal!"

"I'm not creative! I have no idea what to make!"

So many people find cooking a chore. It's no wonder that meal delivery services and meal kits are experiencing a peak in popularity. With meal delivery, all you have to do is heat and eat. What could be simpler? Meal kits are great for people who feel like they like to cook but have no kitchen creativity and must follow a recipe. But after a while, these get very expensive. And what if you don't like what comes in the box?

Healthy food can be delicious + nutritious!

That's why we wrote this book!

After we wrote our first cookbook, "No Excuses! 50 Healthy Ways to ROCK Breakfast!", we were asked over and over again when would we write the follow-up to satisfy their need for amazing lunch and dinner recipes. We tested and tinkered with so many recipes and whittled it down to our favorites. Each recipe had to meet three criteria:

1. Nutritious
2. Delicious
3. Easy to make

As for what kind of "diet" to follow, let's redefine diet once and for all...

cauliflower pizza crust pg. 33

Diet is not something that you are "on" or "off."
Your "diet" is your personal nutrition plan.

Improve your diet,
Improve your health

We challenge those people to look at the other side of the coin - cooking can be a creative outlet with a result that can bring you happiness! When we eat a meal that we truly enjoy, it's because it satisfies us on many levels. It hits multiple taste buds (sweet, sour, salty, bitter, umami), has different textural components (smooth, creamy, crunchy), presents various temperatures, and shows complexity through both brightness and depth of flavor. So, how does one achieve this complexity without being formally trained as a chef? That's where this cookbook comes in! These recipes teach you how to achieve all these levels by using the freshest ingredients and highlighting them with herbs, spices, and acidity.

cauliflower tabbouleh pg. 35

We firmly believe that food can be either the greatest poison or best medicine. In our 20+ years in the nutrition, fitness, and wellness fields, we have seen the power that food has on our health - physically, mentally, and spiritually.

But it's not enough to just tell someone to eat healthier. What does that really mean? Most people hear the word "healthy" and think of plates of plain chicken breast and broccoli and tall glasses of green juice. Not very appetizing or exciting.

No one diet works for everyone

tokyo salmon bowl pg. 28
mediterranean bowl pg. 27

But, there are some diet basics that apply to most everyone.

Fill your plate with Plants

We truly believe that a plant-based diet is key to a healthy life. Plants (fruits, vegetables, whole grains, nuts, seeds, beans, and lentils) are chock-full of fiber and antioxidants which reduce inflammation and risk of disease, such as heart disease, diabetes, cancer, arthritis, and neurodegenerative diseases (dementia and Alzheimer's). There are so many colorful options that it's impossible to get bored with your meals. Make sure to choose a rainbow of colors at each meal. As mentioned earlier, there is no one diet that fits for everyone, so the quantity from each of these food groups will vary from person to person.

Balance each Meal

What we mean is that each meal should have a balance of carbs, protein, and fat in it to promote satiety, balance blood sugar levels, and provide a steady stream of energy. For carbs, choose veggies first and make sure to fill half of your plate with them. Then pick your favorite clean protein (fish, chicken, eggs, beans), and then top it all with an anti-inflammatory fat (avocado, nuts, seeds, coconut oil). Whole grains and fruit should make up a smaller portion of the plate.

No one diet works for everyone

Choose Healthy Fats

Fat is essential to the body. Your brain is approximately 70% fat, and fat makes up every cell membrane and the myelin sheaths that surround your nerves. Getting the right kinds of fat is key to quashing inflammation, balancing your blood sugar levels, and promoting stable energy throughout the day.

- Replace oxidized fats (vegetable oils, margarine, hydrogenated oils, most seed oils, canola oil) with healthy anti-inflammatory fats, such as avocado (and avocado oil), virgin coconut oil, extra virgin olive oil, grass-fed butter, grass-fed ghee, raw nuts, and seeds.

- Get more Omega-3 fats as these have a profound impact on brain health and inflammation. The typical American diet is very high in pro-inflammatory omega-6 fats and too low in omega-3s. Get your omega-3s from wild Alaskan salmon, wild Pacific halibut, sardines, mackerel, and tuna. There are plant forms of omega-3, found in foods like flax and hemp seeds, but these types of omega-3s are not converted well in the body to the active forms. These foods are still important to eat for their fiber and other anti-inflammatory compounds.

"Eat food. Not too much. Mostly plants."

– Michael Pollan, In Defense of Food: An Eater's Manifesto

Hydrate

 If you want high amounts of energy, good digestive function, better mental clarity, and overall improved health, then you need to stay hydrated! Choose water, herbal tea, green tea, even coffee (best to buy organic, certified mold-free) and stay away from soda, juice, foo-foo coffee-blended drinks, and most smoothies as they are high in inflammatory sugar and often bad fats. Keep an insulated water bottle with you at all times to remind you to sip often.

Ditch the Sugar

 Probably more important than anything else is to eliminate added sugars. Sugar tells your body to produce insulin, which is totally normal. Insulin's job is to shuttle the sugar out of the bloodstream and into the cells where they can be burned for energy. Unfortunately, the typical diet is too high in added sugar and foods that quickly convert to sugar, such as refined grains. Plus, sugar is hiding in so many foods, like salad dressing, sauces, and packaged snacks. When insulin is constantly being produced, it becomes a fat-storage hormone which leads to weight gain, diabetes, high blood pressure, elevated cholesterol, and high inflammatory markers. When you switch from processed to homemade meals, you nourish your body with nature's medicine.

client testimonials

"I love food. However, a little over 2 decades ago, I began to learn that many of my favorite foods had a negative effect on my body and the way I felt. As I've transformed my way of eating over the years, I have searched for new recipes that were not only good for me, but also did not require a lot of time, cost, and hard to find ingredients. Erin and Tiffani's recipes not only meet these requirements, but they are also flavorful and delicious! By adding a variety of herbs and natural seasonings, and an abundance of healthy vegetables, they have created recipes that are just the right combination of sweet, salty, and savory. Thank you, Erin and Tiffani, for changing my health—and life—for the better!"

— Wendy L.

I've never been much of a cook. I don't instinctively know what to throw together to make a meal. But I can follow a recipe. Thanks to Erin and Tiffani and their ROCKIN' recipes, cooking has become much easier! Their recipes have been my go-to for years! When I'm unsure about what to make, all I have to do is go to their website and I have so many delicious options! Even better, my son loves everything! From breakfast to dinner to dessert, they've got me covered.

— Kelli S.

Breakfast has always been my favorite meal of the day. So many recipes from Erin and Tiffani's breakfast cookbook have become my default meals. I keep asking them when they're coming out with a lunch and dinner cookbook and now my prayers have been answered! Hooray for recipes for every meal of the day!

— Debra I.

asian lettuce wraps pg. 55

7

kitchen essentials

Spice Aisle

- Pink Himalayan sea salt
- Black pepper
- Lemon pepper
- Garlic powder
- Chili powder
- Cumin
- Smoked paprika
- Crushed red pepper flakes
- Whole coriander seeds
- Ground ginger
- Cinnamon

- Dried Italian seasoning
- Nutritional yeast
- Black or white sesame seeds
- Arrowroot
- Oregano
- Dried basil
- Dried thyme
- Dried marjoram
- Whole nutmeg
- Allspice
- Harissa (Moroccan spice paste)

Equipment:

- Food processor
- High-powered blender (Vitamix™, BlendTec™, Cuisinart™)
- Good knives
- Knife sharpener

- Microplane™ (aka, rasp or fine grater)
- Measuring cups
- Measuring spoons
- Cutting board
- Slow Cooker (CrockPot™)
- Spiralizer

kitchen essentials

Refrigerator:

- Organic plain Greek or Icelandic yogurt
- Sheep's milk Halloumi cheese
- Parmesan cheese
- Goat cheese
- Pastured eggs
- Unsweetened almond milk
- Organic chicken (breasts, thighs)
- Organic ground turkey
- Wild Alaskan Salmon
- Wild Pacific Halibut
- Grass-fed/Grass-finished Beef
- Organic Sprouted Tofu
- Fresh salsa or pico de gallo
- Sweet yellow or white miso

Nuts + Seeds:

- Raw cashews
- Raw almonds
- Raw pecans
- Raw pine nuts
- Raw pepitas
- Raw walnuts
- Chia seeds
- Whole flax seeds

Freezer:

- Organic edamame
- Riced cauliflower
- Chopped spinach

Pantry:

- BPA-free canned beans
- Organic marinara sauce
- BPA-free canned organic tomatoes
- Low-sodium vegetable broth
- Organic canned pumpkin
- Pasture-raised eggs
- Raw almond butter
- Raw cashew butter
- Organic peanut butter
- Organic virgin coconut oil
- Avocado oil
- Extra virgin olive oil
- Low-sodium, gluten-free tamari
- Coconut aminos
- Organic apple cider vinegar (with the "Mother")
- Rice vinegar
- Manitoba Harvest Hemp Hearts©

- Red wine vinegar
- Balsamic glaze
- Toasted sesame oil
- Quinoa
- Raw honey
- Organic tortilla chips
- Salsa verde
- Worcestershire sauce
- Dijon mustard
- Asian sweet chili sauce
- Coconut sugar
- Tahini (sesame seed paste)
- Grade A (Dark & Robust) Maple syrup
- Harissa (Moroccan hot sauce)
- Canned water chestnuts
- Dried tart cherries

chapter 1

I have no time to cook during the week!

Busy days leave little time for cooking each night. Don't worry, we've got you covered. The key to getting a home-cooked dinner on the table every night is to get it all done on the weekend. Pick one ingredient as the star of the week - chicken, ground turkey, quinoa, cauliflower rice - and either make one giant recipe that can be used multiple times (we love leftovers) or scoop out what you need each night and combine it with different ingredients you have on hand. Check out our meal prep cheat sheet for more great tips and ideas.

meal prep cheat sheet
3 days to a week of meals

If time is short during the week, planning, shopping, and prepping your meals during the weekend is key to getting a nutritious and delicious dinner on the table every night. There's no one right way to strategize and plan, but our 3-step plan is a great place to start

friday

Map out your meals for the week

o First, check your calendar for the week. Do you have book club on Monday night? Spin class on Tuesday? Soccer practice on Thursday? Know which days you have to have meals ready to reheat and which days you have 5 or 10 minutes to throw something together with some basic items on hand.
o We love to use old-fashioned pen and paper and use a blank calendar for the week. Then start plugging in meals. Frittata for breakfast Monday, Wednesday, and Friday. Smoothie on Tuesday and Thursday. Last night's dinner for lunch today makes so much sense. It saves you time and energy.

- What kind of meals do you enjoy? We love to go for warm, comforting foods during the cooler months and light, raw, salad-type meals during the warmer months.
- Theme nights might help give you inspiration for planning your meals. Meatless Monday. Taco Tuesday. Breakfast for dinner. Pasta night (with zoodles, naturally). You get the idea.
- Look through your pantry, fridge, and freezer for some ideas. Is that a package of chicken thighs in the freezer? What to do with that bag of red lentils? How about that big bag of rainbow carrots? You can use pretty much any ingredient in any of our recipes. If you don't have one or two items, don't sweat it - substitute it for what you DO have.

saturday

Go shopping

- Rule #1 - Have a list! From the meal plan you sketched out on Friday night, craft your shopping list. If it's not on the list, don't buy it (unless it's just calling your name).
- Go through your seasonings, spices, and sauces to see what's nearly empty or needs to be replaced because it's just too old.
- Stock up on yummy flavored vinegars, delicious oils, fresh herbs, and lots of citrus - these items really add a ton of flavor to your dish, which makes it much more satisfying.

sunday

Cook!

Part of the meal prep practice is deciding if you want to make everything for the whole week, prep some of the meals, or just chop up veggies and organize ingredients to be cooked fresh on the night you want a particular recipe. Many people swear by getting it all done on Sunday so all you have to do each night is just remove from the refrigerator and reheat.

It will take a little more time out of your Sunday, but it leaves the rest of your week with less time in the kitchen. Here are some of our best prep tips:

o Consider cooking double batches of recipes and freezing half which you can then take out in a few weeks and reheat.

o Sheet-pan meals are ideal if you want little to no clean up. Just line a sheet pan with aluminum foil and load it up with your veggies and protein. Season and bake in the oven until done. When cool, load it into containers and toss the foil. No clean up!

o One-pot meals are another great way to cook with little clean up. Sauté your veggies in some avocado oil, add 1/2 cup brown rice or quinoa and cut-up chicken (or other protein), broth, and seasonings, cover with a lid and simmer until done.

o Use your slow-cooker to make soups, chili, or stews. You can load up the slow-cooker in the morning before you leave and set it to cook on LOW for 8-10 hours. When you get home, all you have to do is serve. Make extra so leftovers can be enjoyed for days to come.

shredded chicken

Over the weekend, cook up a whole, organic chicken in a slow-cooker (a.k.a., Crock Pot™) with 1/2 onion, chopped, 2 carrots, chopped, a few sprigs of rosemary and thyme, and 2 cloves garlic, chopped. Cover with filtered water and add 2 Tbs. apple cider vinegar. Cook on low for 12 hours (or longer). When done, carefully remove the chicken (it will fall apart on you) with a pair of tongs. When chicken is cool, separate out the bones and skin and reserve the chicken to a container with a lid, along with the cooked onions and carrots. You will use this chicken during the week in any of these recipes. Strain the soup through a fine mesh strainer/colander into a large container. Cover with a lid and place in the refrigerator. Scrape off any fat that rises to the top.

mango chicken tacos pg. 19

grandma's chicken soup

Serves 2:
6 cups of the reserved broth
1 cup shredded chicken
Reserved onions and carrots
2 cups baby spinach
Seasonal vegetables

. . . .

1. Place the broth, chicken, onions, carrots, and spinach in a pot and heat over medium-low until hot.
2. Ladle into bowls and serve.

Rockin' Tip!

The broth that remains after you cook the chicken is extremely gut healing due to the presence of collagen. Sip on it, replace it instead of water when cooking quinoa, or freeze it in ice cube trays to savor later.

sweet + spicy asian chicken bowl

Nutrition per Serving
244 calories
5 g fat
27 g carbohydrate
3 g fiber
6 g sugar
26 g protein

Serves 4:
1 cup cooked black rice
 (or any kind you have)
2 cups shredded chicken
1 red bell pepper, chopped
1 green onion, chopped
8 sugar snap peas, halved
1/2 cup sliced water chestnuts
2 T Asian BBQ sauce
 (see page 65)
Sesame seeds for garnish

1. Place 1/4 cup black rice and
1/2 cup shredded chicken in each
bowl. Add the veggies and toss with
1-2 Tbs. Asian BBQ sauce. Garnish
with sesame seeds.

cobb salad

Serves 2:

6 cups chopped butter lettuce

4 hard-boiled eggs, chopped

3 slices turkey bacon, cooked
 until crispy and then chopped

2 large avocados, peeled and
 chopped

20 grape tomatoes, halved

2 cups shredded chicken,
 chopped

1/4 cup Lime-Avocado dressing
(see page 69)

1. Divide lettuce among plates or
bowls. Divide remaining toppings
evenly among the plates. Pour 2 Tbs.
dressing on top of each salad and
toss to combine.

Nutrition per Serving
440 calories
27 g fat
25 g carbohydrate
11 g fiber
8 g sugar
34 g protein

mango + chicken tacos

Nutrition per Serving
388 calories
13 g fat
43 g carbohydrate
10 g fiber
14 g sugar
30 g protein

Serves 4:
8 mini organic corn tortillas
(a.k.a., street taco tortillas)
or butter lettuce leaves
1 Tbs. avocado oil
2 cups shredded chicken
1 cup black beans
1/2 tsp. ground cumin
1/2 cup salsa verde
1-2 avocados (depending
on size and amount desired)
or guacamole
1 mango, peeled and cubed
1 cup shredded cabbage

1. Heat oil in a large skillet and add the chicken.
Cook 2-3 minutes or until golden and a little crispy.
2. Place the tortillas or lettuce leaves on plates and
top with the crispy chicken.
3. Mix the beans with cumin and heat in a pot for
3-4 minutes. Spoon on top of chicken.
4. Top each taco with salsa, avocado or guacamole,
mango, and shredded cabbage

ground turkey

Purchase organic ground dark meat turkey for best flavor.
Heat up 1 Tbs. avocado oil in a large skillet and then add 1-2 pounds (depending on the size of your family) ground turkey. Season with pink Himalayan sea salt and lemon pepper. Break up turkey with a wooden spoon or spatula and cook until no longer pink.
Use in the following recipes...

spaghetti squash
bolognese pg. 23

terrific turkey tacos

Serves 4:

8 butter lettuce leaves
 or corn tortillas
1 lb. cooked ground turkey
1 Tbs. avocado oil
1/2 cup onion, chopped
1 red, orange, or yellow bell pepper,
 chopped
1 Tbs. Mexican spice mix (see page 72)
2 cups fresh salsa (whatever kind you like)
Fresh guacamole or 1 large
 avocado, sliced
1/4 cup chopped fresh cilantro

1. Heat oil in a large nonstick skillet over medium-high heat. When hot, add the onion and peppers and season with Mexican spice mix. Saute 5 minutes. Add the cooked ground turkey and 1 1/2 cups salsa and stir everything to combine. Turn heat to low and cook 5 minutes or until turkey is hot.
2. Spoon the turkey into the butter lettuce leaves (or corn tortillas) and top with additional salsa, guacamole (or avocado) and cilantro.

south of the border bowl

Serves 4:
1 Tbs. avocado oil
1 sweet yellow onion, chopped
1 large zucchini, chopped
1 red bell pepper, seeded
 and chopped
1 tsp. ground cumin
1 tsp. chili powder
1 pound ground turkey
1-1 1/2 cups bottled, fresh salsa
1 cup cooked quinoa
1 cup black beans
1 large avocado or guacamole
1/4 cup cotija cheese
1/2 cup chopped cilantro

Nutrition per Serving
484 calories
20 g fat
40 g carbohydrate
11 g fiber
6 g sugar
35 g protein

1. Heat oil in a large skillet. When hot, add the onions, zucchini, and peppers. Season with cumin, chili powder, salt and pepper. Cook 3-4 minutes.
2. Mix the cooked turkey with salsa and heat in a pot until hot.
3. Divide quinoa among 4 bowls. Top with turkey, beans, sautéed veggies, avocado, cheese, and cilantro.

spaghetti squash bolognese

Nutrition per Serving
227 calories
20 g fat
3 g carbohydrate
1 g fiber
2 g sugar
13 g protein

Serves 4:

1 Tbs. avocado oil

2 cups ground turkey

1 spaghetti squash, halved
 and seeded

1 small sweet yellow onion, diced

2 cups cremini mushrooms, diced

2 carrots, diced

4 cloves garlic, minced

2 Tbs. chopped fresh thyme

1 (28 oz.) can San Marzano
 tomatoes (crush or chop them
 if whole)

1 cup cherry tomatoes

Fresh basil

1/4 cup freshly grated
 parmesan cheese

1. Heat the oven to 400F. Line a sheet pan with aluminum foil and coat with a little oil. Place the spaghetti squash, cut side down, onto the sheet pan. Place in the oven and cook 35-45 minutes or until the spaghetti squash is soft to the touch. Remove from oven and let cool.

2. Heat the avocado oil in a large skillet. When hot, add the onions, mushrooms, and carrots. Season with salt and pepper. Sauté 5 minutes. Add the garlic and thyme and sauté 1 minute.

3. Add the canned and fresh tomatoes and 1/2 cup water or vegetable broth. Turn heat to low and simmer the sauce for 15 minutes or until it has thickened. Stir in 2 cups of the ground turkey and simmer another 5 minutes.

4. Serve over spaghetti squash. Top with fresh chopped basil and parmesan cheese.

"The food you eat can either be the safest
and most powerful form of medicine
or the slowest form of poison"

- Ann Wigmore

stuffed peppers

Serves 4:
1/2 lb ground turkey
1 each red, orange and
 yellow bell pepper, halved
 and seeds removed
1 Tbs. avocado oil
1/2 sweet yellow onion,
 chopped
1 zucchini, diced or shredded
1 clove garlic, minced
1 cup crimini mushrooms, diced
1/2 tsp. ground cumin
1/2 tsp. garlic powder
1/2 tsp. smoked paprika
1/4 tsp. pink Himalayan sea salt
1/2 tsp. lemon pepper

1. Heat oil in a large nonstick skillet over medium-high heat. When hot, add the onions, zucchini, garlic, and mushrooms and season with smoked paprika, garlic powder, cumin, salt, and pepper. Cook for 5 minutes.
2. Add the cooked ground turkey to the vegetables and stir to combine. Then fill the pepper halves with turkey mixture. Cover with foil and place in oven for 20 minutes or until peppers start to soften.

Nutrition per Serving
304 calories
14 g fat
20 g carbohydrate
5 g fiber
4 g sugar
25 g protein

quinoa

Make up a pot of quinoa and enjoy all week long. Use 1/4-1/3 cup uncooked quinoa per person, per serving. You will need a fine mesh strainer to rinse the quinoa before you put it in the pot to cook. Use two-parts water (or the homemade broth from when you slow-cooked the chicken) to one-part quinoa, bring to a boil, cover with a lid, and then reduce heat to a simmer. Quinoa will be done in 15 minutes.

Rockin' Tip!

To make any of these recipes vegetarian, just omit the animal protein and increase the amount of beans to 1/2 cup.

mediterranean bowl

Serves 1:
1/3 cup cooked quinoa
1 cup baby spinach
1/2 cup chopped
   cucumber
1/2 cup chopped
   organic red peppers
2 Tbs. chopped
   red onion
1 oz. feta cheese
6 Kalamata olives
3 oz. cooked chicken
2 Tbs. chopped
   fresh mint
2 Tbs. Lemon-Thyme
   Vinaigrette
   (see page 70)

Nutrition per Serving
438 calories
20 g fat
32 g carbohydrate
4 g fiber
6 g sugar
35 g protein

1. Combine all ingredients in a bowl and toss to combine.

tokyo salmon bowl

Nutrition per Serving
582 calories
33 g fat
43 g carbohydrate
10 g fiber
7 g sugar
32 g protein

Serves 1:

1/3 cup cooked quinoa
1/2 cup thinly sliced cucumber
1/2 avocado, peeled
 and cubed
1/2 green onion, chopped
1/2 Tbs. sesame seeds,
1/3 cup organic edamame
3 oz. cooked or raw
 (sashimi-grade) salmon
2 Tbs. Miso-Carrot-Ginger
 dressing (see page 69)

1. Combine all ingredients in a bowl and toss to combine.

Rockin' Tip!

Feel free to swap out the raw or cooked salmon for smoked salmon to get an extra kick of flavor!

pistachio apricot moroccan bowl

Serves 1:

1/3 cup cooked quinoa
2 cups baby spinach
2 dried apricots, chopped
1/3 cup garbanzo beans
3 oz. cooked chicken
1/2 Tbs. Manitoba Harvest Hemp Hearts©

2 Tbs. pistachios, chopped
2 Tbs. Cashew-Harissa dressing
(see page 68)

1. Combine all ingredients in a bowl and toss to combine.

Nutrition per Serving
607 calories
23 g fat
46 g carbohydrate
6 g fiber
15 g sugar
41 g protein

Nutrition per Serving
393 calories
6 g fat
45 g carbohydrate
10 g fiber
10 g sugar
27 g protein

Serves 1:

1/3 cup cooked quinoa
1/4 cup black beans
1/4 cup non-GMO corn
 (fresh or frozen)
2 Tbs. chopped red onion
1/4 cup chopped red pepper
3 oz. cooked shrimp
2 Tbs. Lime-Avocado dressing
(see page 69)

1. Combine all ingredients in a bowl and toss to combine.

Erin says...

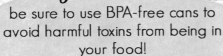

be sure to use BPA-free cans to avoid harmful toxins from being in your food!

cauliflower rice

All you need is a head of cauliflower and a food processor (or cheat and buy the already riced cauliflower in the produce or freezer section). Remove leaves and core from cauliflower and roughly chop the head into large chunks. Place in food processor about 2/3 full. Pulse until pieces are the size of rice. Remove to a bowl and repeat with remaining cauliflower pieces until you have a full bowl of cauliflower rice.

cauliflower pizza crust pg. 33

Serves 4:
1 Tbs. avocado oil
1/2 cup sweet yellow onion, diced
1 zucchini, diced
6 shiitake mushrooms, stemmed and chopped
2 garlic cloves, minced
3 cups cauliflower rice
1 tsp toasted sesame oil
1 Tbs. low-sodium tamari
1 Tbs. rice vinegar
Cracked pepper
2 green onions, chopped
1/2 cup fresh cilantro, chopped
1 Tbs. black sesame seeds

cauliflower fried rice

Tiff says...

add cooked chicken, shrimp, or tofu to make this bowl a complete meal!

Nutrition per Serving
126 calories
7 g fat
14 g carbohydrate
4 g fiber
6 g sugar
5 g protein

1. Place a large non-stick skillet over medium-high heat and place avocado oil in pan. When hot, add the onion, zucchini, and mushrooms and sauté 4 minutes. Add the garlic and sauté 1 minute. Add the cauliflower rice and sauté 3 minutes.
2. Add the sesame oil, tamari, and rice vinegar to the pan and stir to combine with all of the vegetables. Season with black pepper. Stir in the green onion, cilantro, and sesame seeds. Pour into a large serving bowl.

cauliflower pizza crust

Serves 2:
1 head cauliflower,
 riced in the food processor
1 egg
1/4 cup parmesan cheese
1/2 tsp. salt
1/2 tsp. cracked lemon pepper
1/2 tsp. dried rosemary
1/2 tsp. dried oregano
1 Tbs. Manitoba Harvest Hemp Hearts©

Toppings:
1/2 cup Basil-Lemon pesto
(see page 67)
1/2 cup fresh basil
leaves, torn
1 cup grape tomatoes, halved
1 ball fresh mozzarella,
sliced into 6 rounds

Rockin' Tip!

You can substitute the
basil pesto with marinara
sauce and add any
cooked veggies for topping.
Also, play around with
different types of cheese
on top - crumbled goat's
cheese, feta, ricotta.

Nutrition per Serving
265 calories
12 g fat
22 g carbohydrate
9 g fiber
9 g sugar
20 g protein

1. Heat oven to 400F. Line a baking sheet with parchment paper or a silicon baking mat. Set aside.
2. Place your riced cauliflower in a microwave-safe bowl and cook on high for 4 minutes. Let cool for 5 minutes. Pour into a clean kitchen towel and gather the sides of the towel together. Squeeze out all of the water from the cooked cauliflower. You will end up with a small ball of cauliflower.
3. Place the dry cauliflower into a large mixing bowl and add the egg, cheese, salt, pepper, rosemary, oregano, and hemp hearts. Stir until well combined.
4. Pour onto the prepared baking sheet and form into a flat circle (pizza crust). Bake in oven for 10-15 minutes. Remove from oven.
5. Spread the basil pesto sauce on top of the pizza crust. Top with basil, tomatoes, and mozzarella rounds. Return to oven and cook 5 minutes. Remove and serve.

cauliflower tabbouleh

Serves 4:

2 cups riced cauliflower
1/2 cup chopped cilantro
1/2 cup chopped Italian parsley
1/2 cup chopped fresh mint
1/2 cup chopped red onion
1 English cucumber, chopped
20 grape tomatoes, halved
Zest of 1 organic lemon
Juice of 1 lemon
2 Tbs. extra virgin olive oil
1/2 tsp. pink Himalayan sea salt
1 tsp. cracked lemon pepper
1 Tbs. Manitoba Harvest
Hemp Hearts©

Nutrition per Serving
104 calories
7 g fat
8 g carbohydrate
3 g fiber
5 g sugar
3 g protein

1. Into a large mixing bowl place the cauliflower, cilantro, parsley, mint, onion, cucumber, and tomatoes. Stir until well combined. Season with salt and pepper and stir to combine. Mix together the lemon zest, lemon juice, and olive oil. Pour over the mixture and stir until well combined. Sprinkle with hemp hearts. Taste and adjust seasonings to your liking.

chicken + broccoli casserole

Nutrition per Serving
185 calories
8 g fat
10 g carbohydrate
3 g fiber
3 g sugar
22 g protein

Serves 6:
2 cups riced cauliflower
2 cups chopped broccoli
1/2 cup chopped sweet
   yellow onion
3/4 cup cottage cheese,
   blended until smooth
1 cup shredded cheese,
   divided (pick your
   favorite variety)
1 tsp. garlic powder
2 cups shredded chicken
breast

1. Heat oven to 350F. Prepare an 8x8-inch glass baking dish by rubbing with avocado oil or coating with avocado oil cooking spray and set aside.

2. Combine the cauliflower, broccoli, onion, cottage cheese, and half of the shredded cheese in a large mixing bowl and mix until well blended. Sprinkle with garlic powder and stir in the chicken.

3. Pour into the baking dish and sprinkle the top with remaining cheese. Cover with foil and bake 25 minutes. Remove and let cool. Cut into 6 generous pieces.

chapter 2

I don't like doing dishes!

honey chili lime salmon pg. 42

Don't like to clean up and do dishes? Neither do we! Just line a sheet pan with aluminum foil and place all of the ingredients on the pan. Cook, serve, and toss the aluminum foil in the trash - the dishes are done!

pesto chicken + vegetables

Nutrition per Serving
330 calories
9 g fat
34 g carbohydrate
6 g fiber
3 g sugar
33 g protein

1 batch Basil-Lemon Pesto (see page 67)
1 lb. chicken breast tenders
4 red potatoes, thinly sliced
1 cup grape tomatoes
1 bunch asparagus, ends trimmed
Pink Himalayan sea salt
Cracked lemon pepper

1. Heat oven to 375F. Line a baking sheet with aluminum foil.
2. Place chicken and vegetables on the baking sheet. Season vegetables with salt and pepper.
3. Spoon pesto over the chicken. Place in the oven and bake for 15 minutes, or until chicken is no longer pink inside.

Erin says... this basil-lemon pesto ROCKS! It works great on chicken, fish, eggs, pasta, veggies, and pizza!

steak fajitas

Serves 4:

1 lb. flank steak, sliced against
  the grain into 1/2-inch strips
1 1/2 Tbs. Mexican spice blend
  (see page 72)
2 cloves garlic, minced
1/2 tsp. sea salt
1/2 tsp. lemon pepper
2 Tbs. avocado oil
1 red bell pepper, sliced into thin strips

1 orange bell pepper, sliced into thin strips
1 sweet onion, sliced into thin strips
Fresh chopped cilantro
Lime wedges
Optional: sour cream or plain Greek yogurt
8 mini corn tortillas

Tiff says...

don't be afraid of using a generous amount
of the spice blend - it really lends a ton of
flavor to the dish along with a big squeeze of
lime on the finished dish.

Nutrition per Serving
339 calories
14 g fat
24 g carbohydrate
6 g fiber
7 g sugar
28 g protein

1. Heat oven to 400F. Line a sheet pan with foil.
2. Combine Mexican blend, chopped garlic, salt, pepper, and oil in a bowl and whisk together.
3. Place steak and vegetables on sheet pan in a single layer. Pour seasoned oil over the meat and vegetables and use your hands to spread over everything. Place sheet pan in oven and bake for 10-15 minutes, to your level of meat doneness.
4. While meat and veggies are cooking, heat the tortillas.
5. Remove sheet pan from oven. Serve 2 tortillas per person. Divide meat and vegetables onto each tortilla, garnish with cilantro and serve with lime wedges. Top with sour cream (if so desired).

cashew chicken

Nutrition per Serving
282 calories
7 g fat
23 g carbohydrate
5 g fiber
11 g sugar
31 g protein

Serves 4:
1 lb. chicken breast
  tenders, cut into
  1-inch chunks
1 head broccoli, cut
  into florets
1 red bell pepper, cut
  into chunks
1/2 cup raw cashews

Teriyaki sauce:
1/4 c low-sodium
  tamari or coconut
  aminos
2 Tbs. rice vinegar
1 Tbs. raw honey
1 clove garlic, minced
1/2 tsp. grated ginger
1/2 Tbs. arrowroot

1. Heat oven to 375F. Line a sheet pan with foil or parchment paper. Place chicken and vegetables onto sheet pan.
2. Whisk together the sauce ingredients and pour half of the sauce over the chicken and vegetables. Place sheet pan in oven and bake 10-12 minutes.
3. While the food is cooking, heat the remaining sauce in the microwave on high for 1 minute.
4. Remove from the oven and drizzle with remaining sauce. Serve with brown rice.

honey chili lime salmon

Serves 4:

1 Tbs. raw honey
Juice of 2 limes
1/4 tsp. red chili flakes
 (adjust to your level
 of spice)
2 Tbs. avocado oil
2 Tbs. chopped cilantro
Pinch pink sea salt
Cracked black pepper
4 (4 oz.) fillets wild
 Alaskan salmon
1 red bell pepper,
 chopped
1 orange bell pepper,
 chopped
1/2 sweet yellow onion,
 chopped

Nutrition per Serving
333 calories
21 g fat
9 g carbohydrate
1 g fiber
7 g sugar
26 g protein

1. Heat oven to broil. Line a sheet pan with foil. Place salmon and vegetables on sheet pan.
2. Whisk together honey, lime juice, chili flakes, oil, cilantro, salt, and pepper in a bowl. Pour over the salmon and vegetables.
3. Place in oven under broiler for 4 minutes. Reset oven to bake at 375F and cook for 5 more minutes.

chapter 3

halibut lemon skillet pg. 49

I don't have tons of ingredients!

Don't have a lot of ingredients in the house? Don't want to spend a lot of time prepping dinner? No problem - these recipes are easy, healthy and quick!

chicken enchilada casserole

Nutrition per Serving
218 calories
11 g fat
17 g carbohydrate
2 g fiber
8 g sugar
13 g protein

Serves 4:

2 cups tortilla chips, crushed

1 zucchini, shredded

1 container chunky salsa

1/2 cup shredded cheddar cheese

2 cups shredded chicken

1/2 Tbs. Mexican spice blend (see page 72)

1. Heat oven to 350F.
2. Combine all ingredients in a large mixing bowl and then transfer to an 8x8-inch glass baking dish. Cover with foil and place in oven. Bake 20 minutes.
3. Remove from oven and serve. Cut into 4 generous servings.

Tiff says...

if you end up with bags of tortilla chip dust like we do, don't trash them! Save them in a zip-top bag until you have enough to make this casserole. We've even done this using different types of chips and it turns out great!

lemony zoodles with fried halloumi

Nutrition per Serving
227 calories
20 g fat
3 g carbohydrate
1 g fiber
2 g sugar
13 g protein

Serves 4:
2 zucchinis, spiralized
Pink sea salt
1 Tbs. avocado oil
8 oz. Halloumi
 (sheep's milk) cheese
1/2 tsp. ground coriander
1/4 tsp. cumin
Lemon pepper
Juice of 1/2 lemon
Fresh chopped cilantro
 or basil (garnish)

Rockin' Tip!

Halloumi is a hard cheese that holds it's shape when cooked. Hot, salty, and cheesy goodness!

. . . .

1. Spiralize zucchini and place on paper towels. Sprinkle with salt and let sit 10 minutes. Then blot dry.

2. Remove the halloumi from the package and blot dry.
Slice the halloumi in half and then slice each half into 8 pieces, for a total of 16 pieces.

3. Heat the oil in a large non-stick pan. When hot, add the halloumi and let cook until golden on the bottom, about 4 minutes. Flip and let cook another 4 minutes. Remove to a plate. Add the zucchini to the same pan and season with coriander, cumin, and a few grinds of lemon pepper. Let cook 2 minutes. Add the juice of 1/2 lemon.

4. Place the zucchini in a bowl and top with 4 Halloumi slices and some chopped herbs.

"To eat is a necessity,
but to eat intelligently is an art."

- Francois La Rochefoucald

skillet turkey meatballs

(see page 72)

Rockin' Tip!
When using dried herbs, wake them up by rubbing them between your palms before adding them to the recipe. By crushing them, you release some of their essential oils.

• • • • • • • • • • • • • • • • • • •

Serves 4:

1 lb. ground organic turkey

1 Tbs. dried Italian blend
  (see page 72)

Salt and pepper

1 Tbs. worcestershire
  sauce

1 egg, beaten

1/4 cup ground flax seed

1 Tbs. avocado oil

1 jar (16 oz.) marinara sauce

1/3 cup parmesan cheese

1 Tbs. Manitoba Harvest
  Hemp Hearts©

Nutrition per Serving
356 calories
20 g fat
16 g carbohydrate
5 g fiber
9 g sugar
30 g protein

Rockin' Tip!

Buy whole flaxseeds and grind them fresh to prevent them from going rancid. Store in the refrigerator for freshness.

1. Combine turkey, Italian seasoning, worcestershire sauce, egg, hemp hearts, and flax seed in a large mixing bowl and use your hands to mix everything together. Use a small ice cream scoop to portion out the meatballs.

2. Heat oil in a large non-stick pan, When hot, add the meatballs and cook 2 minutes. Flip with a spatula and cook 2 more minutes. Pour the sauce over the meatballs and cover the pan with a lid. Lower heat to simmer and cook 20 minutes.

3. Remove lid and add grated parmesan cheese and allow to melt.

4. Serve with brown-rice spaghetti, zoodles, or spaghetti squash.

"No one is born a great cook, one learns by doing"

- Julia Child

halibut lemon skillet

Serves 4:

1 Tbs. avocado oil

1 lb. halibut, cut into
 4 pieces

Pinch each pink sea salt
 and lemon pepper

1/2 cup quinoa, rinsed

1 cup low-sodium
 vegetable broth

8 brussels sprouts, quartered

Juice of 1 lemon + 1 lemon,
 sliced into thin rounds

Nutrition per Serving
262 calories
7 g fat
19 g carbohydrate
3 g fiber
2 g sugar
28 g protein

1. Heat oil in a medium nonstick skillet over medium high heat. Add the brussels sprouts and sauté 5 minutes. Add the quinoa, broth, and lemon slices. Bring to a boil and then reduce heat to low; cover with a lid and simmer for 14 minutes.

2. Heat a large nonstick pan over medium heat. When hot, add the halibut pieces and season with salt and pepper. Cook 4 minutes; flip and cook an additional 4 minutes.

3. Serve 1 piece halibut with 1/4 of the quinoa and brussels sprouts; squeeze lemon juice over the fish.

49

steak kabobs

Nutrition per Serving
298 calories
11 g fat
8 g carbohydrate
2 g fiber
4 g sugar
24 g protein

Serves 4:

1 lb. sirloin steak,
 cut into 1 1/2 -inch cubes
1 sweet yellow onion,
 cut into 1-inch chunks
2 zucchini, cut into
 1-inch chunks
2 Tbs. avocado oil
1/2 tbs. ground coriander
1/4 tsp. pink Himalayan
 sea salt
1/2 tsp. cracked pepper
Juice of 1 lemon

1. Thread steak, onion and zucchini onto metal skewers. Rub with oil and season with coriander, salt, and pepper.
2. Heat an indoor grill pan or outdoor grill or BBQ. When hot, place the skewers on the grill and cook 1-2 minutes per side for a total of 6-8 minutes, depending on your desired doneness of meat. Squeeze lemon juice over the skewers and serve.

Erin says...

grass-fed, grass finished beef is the cleanest and healthiest type of beef available. Most grocery stores now carry it or you can order it online.

I don't have tons of ingredients! 50

chapter 4

I don't have any protein on hand!

asian lettuce wraps pg. 55

I don't have any protein in the house! How can I make dinner? It's funny how we seem to think that all meals must center around protein, like chicken, turkey, fish, or beef. You'll get plenty of protein in these vegetarian meals. If you don't have any animal protein in the fridge or freezer, or if you enjoy Meatless Monday© or are a part-time vegetarian, these recipes are for you! A plant-based diet is key to reducing inflammation and lowering your risk of obesity, diabetes, heart disease, and cancer. As we like to tell our clients, "Eat a Rainbow of veggies every day!"

orange tofu stir fry

Serves 4:

1 tsp. toasted sesame oil
1 block extra firm sprouted
  tofu, drained and cubed
1 red bell pepper, sliced thin
1/4 sweet yellow onion,
  chopped
6 shiitake mushrooms,
  stemmed and sliced thin
2 cups baby spinach
2 Tbs. Orange Sauce
  (see page 66), plus more
  for serving
1 green onion, chopped
1/2 Tbs. black sesame seeds
2 cups cooked quinoa

1. Heat the oil in a large nonstick pan. When hot, add the tofu and sauté until golden on all sides. Add the bell peppers, onions, and mushrooms and sauté 3 minutes. Then add the baby spinach and sauté 1 minute. Add 2 Tbs. Orange Sauce and stir to coat all the vegetables.

2. Pour the stir fry into a serving dish and sprinkle with green onions and sesame seeds. Serve with 1/2 cup quinoa.

Nutrition per Serving
296 calories
10 g fat
30 g carbohydrate
4 g fiber
6 g sugar
20 g protein

green shakshuka

Serves 4:

3 cups baby greens
(we used a mix of kale,
chard, and spinach)
1/2 jalapeno, seeds and
ribs removed
1 tsp. raw honey
1 tsp. cumin
1 tsp. smoked paprika
1/2 cup cilantro
1/2 Tbs. lemon zest
1/2 Tbs. Manitoba Harvest
Hemp Hearts©

2 Tbs. avocado oil
1/2 tsp. pink Himalayan sea salt
1/2 tsp. cracked lemon pepper
1/2 sweet yellow onion, diced
3 cups baby greens
1 chopped garlic clove
4 pasture-raised eggs
Pinch sea salt
1/2 tsp. black pepper
Juice of 1/2 lemon

Nutrition per Serving
162 calories
12 g fat
8 g carbohydrate
2 g fiber
3 g sugar
7 g protein

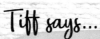

Tiff says...

this green shakshuka is absolutely addictive! The combination of the greens, spices, and lemon just pop!

1. Place the baby greens, jalapeno, honey, cumin, paprika, cilantro, lemon zest, avocado oil, salt and pepper in a food processor. Pulse to break down greens and then run the machine to achieve an almost-smooth consistency.

2. Heat 1 Tbs. avocado oil in a large nonstick pan; when hot, add in greens with onions and garlic and sauté for 2 minutes. Add the sauce and sauté 1 minute. Make 4 wells in the sauce and crack an egg into each well. Cover the pan and cook until the egg whites are set, about 4 minutes (depending on how runny you like your egg). Remove lid and season eggs with salt and pepper. Squeeze 1/2 lemon over the contents of the pan and sprinkle with hemp hearts.

3. Divide greens and eggs onto 4 plates.

"Our food should be our medicine
& our medicine should be our food."

- Hippocrates

asian lettuce wraps

Serves 4:

1 block extra-firm sprouted tofu, drained and mashed with a fork
1 tsp. toasted sesame oil
1 Japanese eggplant, diced
1 red bell pepper, diced
1/2 sweet yellow onion, diced
1 clove garlic, minced
1 (4 oz.) can water chestnuts, chopped
2 Tbs. Asian BBQ sauce (see page 65)
8 butter lettuce leaves
1/4 cup chopped fresh cilantro
1 Tbs. black or white sesame seeds

Nutrition per Serving
178 calories
8 g fat
16 g carbohydrate
7 g fiber
7 g sugar
12 g protein

1.   Heat oil in a large non-stick skillet over medium-high heat. Add the eggplant, red bell pepper, and onion and sauté 5 minutes. Add the garlic and cook 1 minute. Add the tofu and water chestnuts and sauté 3 minutes.

2.   Add the sauce and stir to coat. Fold in the cilantro and sesame seeds. Divide among the lettuce leaves and serve with additional sauce, if needed.

chapter 5

I don't want to have a heavy meal!

crunchy detox salad pg. 63

If you don't love feeling weighed down after a meal, or if the weather is hot, a cool and refreshing salad is the way to go. And no, not the boring lettuce, cucumber, tomato garden salad. We're talking salads with personality! Load up whatever veggies you have on hand (raw or roasted) for clean carbs and belly-filling fiber, add in some clean protein (salmon, shrimp, chicken, tofu, beans), and balance it all out with some satiating fat (avocado, nuts, seeds, extra virgin olive oil). For a bonus that will really make your salad sing, add a little bit of fruit and/or fresh herbs. You're going to love salad again!

roasted golden beet + arugula salad

Serves 2:
1 large organic gold beet
2 oz. goat cheese
1 tsp. avocado oil
1 tsp. raw honey
1/8 tsp. Smoked paprika
1/8 tsp. garlic powder
Pinch Pink Himalayan sea salt
1/4 cup raw walnuts
3 cups baby arugula
1/4 cup pomegranate seeds
6 oz. grilled chicken breast,
  chopped
2 Tbs. balsamic glaze

Nutrition per Serving
393 calories
21 g fat
31 g carbohydrate
4 g fiber
22 g sugar
27 g protein

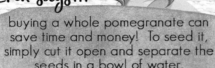

Erin says...

buying a whole pomegranate can save time and money! To seed it, simply cut it open and separate the seeds in a bowl of water.

1. Heat oven to 375F. Line a sheet pan with aluminum foil and coat with a small amount of avocado oil. Peel the beet and slice into 1/4-inch thick rounds. Place on baking sheet and place in oven. Roast until tender, about 15-20 minutes. Remove from oven and let cool.

2. While beets are cooking, mix together the oil, honey, paprika, garlic powder, and salt in a small bowl. Add the walnuts and toss to coat. Heat a small pan over low heat and add the walnuts to the pan. Cook 5 minutes, stirring every 30 seconds to prevent burning. Remove from the pan and let cool on a plate.

3. Place the arugula onto 2 plates. Top each plate with half of the beets, pomegranate seeds, goat cheese, walnuts, and chicken. Drizzle with balsamic glaze.

cold shrimp pad thai salad

Nutrition per Serving
384 calories
21 g fat
27 g carbohydrate
6 g fiber
17 g sugar
36 g protein

Serves 2:
2 zucchini, spiralized or
  cut into ribbons using
  a vegetable peeler
2 carrots, peeled into ribbons
2 green onions, chopped
3 Tbs. chopped raw,
  organic peanuts
  (or any nut you prefer)
1/2 Tbs. sesame seeds
1/4 cup fresh cilantro,
  chopped
1/2 Tbs. Manitoba Harvest
  Hemp Hearts©
1 Tbs. avocado oil
8 oz. fresh or frozen shrimp,
  peeled and deveined
Pinch pink Himalayan sea salt
1/2 tsp. cracked lemon pepper
Juice of 1/2 lime
3 Tbs. Thai Peanut Dressing
  (see page 66)

1. Place the zucchini, carrots, green onions, peanuts, sesame seeds, hemp hearts, and cilantro in a large mixing bowl. Toss with the dressing and set aside.
2. Heat avocado oil in a large non-stick pan over medium high heat. When hot, add the shrimp, season with salt and pepper. Cook 2 minutes; flip, add lime juice and cook 2 more minutes. Remove to a cutting board and chop when cool.
3. Add the warm shrimp to the bowl and toss to combine everything.

Tiff says...
we love using a spiralizer for this salad! If you don't have one, just use a vegetable peeler to make long ribbons.

maple-rosemary brussels sprout salad

Serves 2:

1 Tbs. avocado oil
1 cup shaved brussels sprouts
1/4 cup chopped red onion
 or shallot
2 carrots, peeled and chopped
Pinch pink Himalayan sea salt
1/2 tsp. cracked lemon pepper
1/4 cup dried tart cherries
2 Tbs. Manitoba Harvest Hemp Hearts©
4 cups mixed greens
2 (4 oz.) grilled chicken breasts,
 chopped
3 Tbs. Maple-Rosemary Dressing
 (see page 71)

1. Heat avocado oil in a large nonstick pan over medium-high heat. When hot, add the brussels sprouts, onion, and carrots. Season with salt and pepper and sauté 6-7 minutes. Pour half of the dressing into the pan and toss to coat the vegetables. Let cool 5 minutes.

2. Place the mixed greens in a salad bowl and add the warm vegetables, tart cherries, hemp hearts, and chopped chicken. Toss the salad to evenly mix everything and add additional dressing, if desired.

I don't want to have a heavy meal! 60

salmon poke bowl

Serves 1:
4 oz. wild Alaskan salmon (fresh or frozen)
1 cup thinly sliced cucumber
1/2 avocado, pitted and cubed
2 Tbs. thinly sliced white onion
1 green onion, chopped
2 Tbs. fresh cilantro, chopped
1 Tbs. seasoned rice vinegar
1 Tbs. low-sodium tamari or coconut aminos
1/4 tsp. red pepper flakes
Optional:
  1 tsp. sesame seeds
  1 cup baby greens

Rockin' Tip!

Wild Alaskan salmon season is mid-May to the beginning of October. Out of season, you can buy it frozen. Stay away from Atlantic farm-raised salmon.

Nutrition per Serving
386 calories
22 g fat
19 g carbohydrate
7 g fiber
28 g protein

"*Good nutrition creates health in all areas of our existence. All parts are interconnected.*"

– T. Collin Campbelll

1. Place salmon, cucumber, avocado, onion, green onion, and cilantro in a mixing bowl. Combine the vinegar, tamari and optional red pepper flakes in a small bowl. Pour over the salmon mixture and toss everything to coat. Sprinkle with sesame seeds.
2. Place salad greens in a bowl and top with the salmon mixture.

Erin says...

choose sashimi-grade salmon if you are going to consume it raw or you can cook the salmon.

crunchy detox salad

Serves 2:
3 cups organic baby kale
1/2 cup cooked quinoa
1/2 cup organic edamame
1/2 cup chopped pear
1/4 cup pomegranate seeds
1/4 cup chopped raw almonds
1 avocado, pitted and cubed
3 Tbs. Miso-Carrot-Ginger dressing (see page 69)

1. Combine all ingredients in a large mixing bowl. Toss with the dressing and serve.

Nutrition per Serving
500 calories
33 g fat
42 g carbohydrate
15 g fiber
14 g sugar
18 g protein

chapter 6

I can't season things well!

maple rosemary dressing pg. 71

Most salad dressings, sauces, and spice packets are full of sugar, salt, and chemicals - not exactly what we'd call clean. Making your own is so simple and delicious. Once you make your own, you'll wonder why you ever bought the bottled stuff! You can double the amounts called for to make a larger batch that will stay well in the fridge for 2-3 weeks.

sauces

asian bbq sauce

Makes 4 servings (2 Tbs each):
1 Tbs. low-sodium gluten-free tamari
  (or coconut aminos)
2 tsp. Asian sweet chili sauce
1 Tbs. coconut sugar
1/2 tsp. toasted sesame oil
1/4 tsp. crushed red pepper
1 tsp. arrowroot (only add this if
  the sauce is being used in a
  cooked dish; omit for a dressing)

1. Combine all ingredients in a jar and seal
with a lid. Shake vigorously to combine.

Nutrition per Serving
26 calories
1 g fat
4 g carbohydrate
0 g fiber
4 g sugar
1 g protein

65

orange sauce

Makes 4 servings (2 Tbs. each):
1 Tbs. low-sodium gluten-free tamari
 (or coconut aminos)
2 tsp. Asian sweet chili sauce
1 Tbs. coconut sugar
1/2 tsp. toasted sesame oil
1/4 tsp. crushed red pepper
1 tsp. arrowroot
zest and juice of 1 organic orange

1. Combine all ingredients in a jar and seal with a lid. Shake to combine. Use in any stir-fry for a sweet and spicy Asian sauce.

Nutrition per Serving
36 calories
1 g fat
7 g carbohydrate
0 g fiber
6 g sugar
1 g protein

thai peanut sauce –

You can use raw almond butter, cashew butter, or even sunflower seed butter in place of the peanut butter.

Makes 4 servings (2 Tbs. each):
2 T organic peanut butter
2 T low-sodium tamari
 or coconut aminos
2 T grated fresh ginger
1 T toasted sesame oil
2 T raw honey
1/8 tsp red pepper flakes
1/2 lime, juiced

1. Combine all ingredients in a jar and seal with a lid. Shake to combine. Store in the refrigerator until ready to use.

Nutrition per Serving
130 calories
8 g fat
13 g carbohydrate
1 g fiber
10 g sugar
2 g protein

basil-lemon pesto –

To toast the pine nuts (or any raw nut), place in a pan over low heat on the stove. Shake pan every 30 seconds to prevent them from burning. Total cook time is 3-4 minutes.

Makes 4 servings (2 Tbs. each):
16 large basil leaves
1 clove garlic, minced
zest and juice of 1 organic lemon
2 Tbs. raw pine nuts, toasted
1 Tbs. Manitoba Harvest Hemp Hearts©
1 Tbs. parmesan cheese
 or nutritional yeast
1/4 tsp. lemon pepper
2 Tbs. extra-virgin olive oil

Nutrition per Serving
115 calories
11 g fat
3 g carbohydrate
1 g fiber
1 g sugar
2 g protein

1. Place all ingredients except oil into a food processor and blend until smooth. With the processor running, slowly stream in the oil until mixture is well-blended.

pesto chicken + vegetables pg. 38

dressings

cashew-harissa
Buy raw nuts whenever you can - roasted nuts are usually cooked in a pro-inflammatory oil.

Makes 4 servings (2 Tbs. each):
1 cup raw cashews
1/4 cup water (or more, if necessary)
1 Tbs. harissa
1 Tbs. honey
Juice of 1 lemon

1. Soak the cashews in filtered water for at least 1 hour. Then drain off the water and give the cashews a quick rinse. Place the cashews in a food processor with the remaining ingredients and blend until smooth, adding 1 Tbs. water at a time until the desired consistency is achieved.

miso-carrot-ginger - This dressing will thicken in the fridge. Thin it out with more rice vinegar or water.

Makes 4 servings (2 Tbs. each):
3 Tbs. sweet yellow miso paste
2 Tbs. avocado oil
2 Tbs. chopped carrot
1 tsp. finely grated fresh ginger

1 Tbs. rice vinegar
2 tsp. toasted sesame oil
2 tsp. raw honey
2 Tbs. water
1 Tbs. black sesame seeds

Nutrition per Serving
136 calories
11 g fat
8 g carbohydrate
1 g fiber
6 g sugar
2 g protein

1. Combine all ingredients except sesame seeds in a food processor and blend until smooth. Stir in sesame seeds. Pour into a jar with a lid and keep in the refrigerator until ready to use.

lime-avocado - Always buy organic citrus fruit when using the zest!

Makes 4 servings (2 Tbs. each):
Juice of 2 limes
Zest of 1 organic lime
1/4 cup chopped fresh cilantro
1 large avocado
1/2 Tbs. red wine vinegar
1 tsp. raw honey

1. Place all ingredients in the bowl of a small food processor. Blend until smooth.
2. Pour into a jar with a lid and keep in the refrigerator until ready to use. You can thin it out with some water if it gets too thick.

Nutrition per Serving
40 calories
3 g fat
5 g carbohydrate
1 g fiber
2 g sugar
0 g protein

cobb salad pg. 18

lemon-thyme vinaigrette –

The zest of citrus fruits contain essential oils and powerful antioxidants. Adding the zest to any recipe will really punch up the flavor!

Makes 4 servings (2 Tbs. each):
Juice of 2 lemons
Zest of 1 organic lemon
2 Tbs. EVOO or avocado oil
2 Tbs. diced shallots
1 tsp. Dijon mustard
1 Tbs. chopped fresh thyme
1/4 tsp. cracked lemon pepper

1. Place all ingredients into a jar and seal with the lid. Shake vigorously until well blended. Store in the refrigerator until ready to use. Shake before using.

Nutrition per Serving
71 calories
7 g fat
5 g carbohydrate
0 g fiber
1 g sugar
0 g protein

red wine vinaigrette –

When choosing EVOO, look on the bottle or label for the harvest date and choose one with the newest date to ensure freshness.

Makes 4 servings (2 Tbs. each):
2 Tbs. red wine vinegar
2 Tbs. Extra virgin olive oil (EVOO)
1/2 Tbs. Dijon mustard
Pinch pink Himalayan sea salt
1/4 tsp. cracked lemon pepper
1 tsp. raw honey

Nutrition per Serving
68 calories
7 g fat
1 g carbohydrate
0 g fiber
1 g sugar
0 g protein

1. Combine all ingredients in a jar and seal with lid. Shake vigorously until well combined. Place in refrigerator until serving. Shake before using, as oil and vinegar will likely separate.

miso-tahini –
This dressing will thicken in the fridge. Thin it out with more rice vinegar or water.

Makes 4 servings (2 Tbs. each):
2 tbs. sweet yellow or white miso
2 tbs. tahini (sesame paste)
1 tbs. low-sodium tamari
2 tbs. seasoned rice vinegar

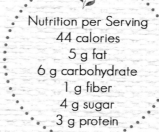

Nutrition per Serving
44 calories
5 g fat
6 g carbohydrate
1 g fiber
4 g sugar
3 g protein

1. Combine all ingredients in a bowl and whisk to combine. You may want to add more vinegar or some water to thin it out. It will get thick the longer it sits in the refrigerator.
2. Pour into a jar with a lid and keep in the refrigerator until ready to use.

maple rosemary –
Always buy the unfiltered apple cider vinegar that looks cloudy at the bottom. This is called the "mother." Apple cider vinegar helps with digestion.

Makes 4 servings (2 Tbs. each):
1 tsp. chopped fresh rosemary
1 Tbs. maple syrup (Grade A dark amber)
2 Tbs. raw smooth almond butter
1 Tbs. extra virgin olive oil or avocado oil
2 Tbs. apple cider vinegar (shake before using)

1. Place all ingredients in a jar and seal with a lid. Shake vigorously until well blended. You can also do this in a bowl and combine with a whisk.

Nutrition per Serving
92 calories
8 g fat
5 g carbohydrate
1 g fiber
4 g sugar
2 g protein

71

maple rosemary brussels sprout salad pg. 60

essential spice blends

pumpkin pie spice

2 Tbs. cinnamon
1/2 tsp. ginger
1/2 tsp. nutmeg
1/2 tsp. allspice

all-purpose seasoning

2 Tbs. onion powder
2 Tbs. garlic powder
1/2 tsp. pink salt
1/2 tsp. lemon pepper

italian blend

1 Tbs. oregano
1 Tbs. basil
1 Tba. thyme
1/2 Tbs. marjoram
1 Tbs. coriander

mexican blend

2 Tbs. ground cumin
2 Tbs. chili powder
1 Tbs. smoked paprika
1 Tbs. garlic powder

about us

We wear many hats each day – mom, wife, daughter, sister, cousin, nutritionist, health coach, cook, chauffeur, writer, doctor, therapist, banker, laundress – you get the idea. Some of these jobs we enjoy with much more gusto than others. But any time we have the opportunity to make a difference in someone else's life is what really drives us. One of the best ways we can help someone is by nourishing them with food that is both nutritious and delicious. When you are both satiated and satisfied, you achieve a level of contentment that's hard to match. If you are just full, but not satisfied, you will continue to look for more food. If you are satisfied but not full, you'll get hungry much more quickly. Our recipes are designed so you achieve both – the perfect way to nourish your mind, body, and spirit.

xo,

Tiff and Erin

acknowledgements

There are so many people we want to thank for supporting us in pouring our time and passion into this book. Without their patience, understanding and expertise, this book could not have gone from our heart to paper.

Thank you to:

Our families:
Erin's family: Hubby Scott and awesome foursome kids, Eric, Ryan, Alex, and Jax, who taste-tested so many recipes.
Tiffani's family: Husband Dan and kids, Dylan, Emily, and Riley who inspired many of these recipes.

Wendy McElfish for shooting the beautiful and mouth-watering photographs!

Breanne Zebrowski, our amazing intern and graphic designer, who slaved for hours to make this cookbook dream come true!

Our parents, Denise and Ernie, Suzi and Pops, Jimmy and Sally, for raising us, loving us, supporting us, and putting us through school so we could become Registered Dietitian Nutritionists!

Everyone who has attended Erin's cooking classes, from which many of these recipes have been inspired!

recipe index

enjoy + bon appétit!

— Erin + Tiff

Food Photographer:
Wendy McElfish
Graphic Designer:
Breanne Zebrowski
Illustrator:
Greta Schimmel

Visit the U Rock Girl website at
www.urockgirl.com
Twitter
@urockgirl
Instagram
@u_rock_girl
Facebook
www.facebook.com/URockGirl.URG
Youtube
www.youtube.com/urockgirltv
Email
contactus@urockgirl.com

Textured background image -

<a href="https://www.freepik.com/free-photos-vectors/background">Background image created by Aopsan - Freepik.com</a>

89483306R00046

Made in the USA
San Bernardino, CA
26 September 2018